Santa Fe & Taos
A History in Postcards

Mary L. Martin
and Ginny Parfitt

Schiffer Publishing Ltd
4880 Lower Valley Road, Atglen, PA 19310 USA

Dedication

To Dylan, Jaime, and Grace—consummate travelers from the word 'go.'

Other Schiffer Books by Mary L. Martin and Ginny Parfitt
Memories of Memphis: A History in Postcards

Other Schiffer Books on Related Subjects
Bandelier National Monument: Home of the Ancestral Pueblo People, by John and Cassidy Olson
Cape Cod Memories: An Illustrated History in Postcards, by Mary L. Martin and Karen Choppa
Greetings from Havre de Grace, by David Craig and Mary L. Martin
Greetings from New Orleans: A History in Postcards, by Mary L. Martin and Tina Skinner
Greetings from Ohio: Vintage Postcards 1900-1960s, by Robert Reed
Greetings from Savannah, by Mary L. Martin, Tina Skinner, and Nathaniel Wolfgang-Price
Hawaii Remembered: Postcards from Paradise, by Tina Skinner, Mary L. Martin, and Nathanial Wolfgang-Price
Newport News: A Vintage Postcard Tour, by Harold Cones and John Bryant
Santa Fe & Surrounds, by John and Cassidy Olson

Library of Congress Control Number: 2006924360

Designed by Mark David Bowyer
Type set in Benguiat Bk BT / Arrus BT

ISBN: 0-7643-2384-9
Printed in China

Published by Schiffer Publishing Ltd.
4880 Lower Valley Road
Atglen, PA 19310
Phone: (610) 593-1777; Fax: (610) 593-2002
E-mail: Info@schifferbooks.com

In Europe, Schiffer books are distributed by
Bushwood Books
6 Marksbury Ave.
Kew Gardens
Surrey TW9 4JF England
Phone: 44 (0) 20 8392-8585; Fax: 44 (0) 20 8392-9876
E-mail: info@bushwoodbooks.co.uk
Website: www.bushwoodbooks.co.uk
Free postage in the U.K., Europe; air mail at cost.

Contents

Introduction

At first glance, it is easy to see why Santa Fe, New Mexico is called "The City Different," as it is a city different from any other in the United States of America. In 1958, the city passed a zoning code making it mandatory that any building constructed in the city have some elements of the famous "Santa Fe style," a mixture of Spanish and Pueblo architectural elements. Santa Fe is also home to sizable Native American and Hispanic populations, whose distinctive art and culture further contribute to the city's unique atmosphere.

Santa Fe has been a destination for travelers since William Becknell first traveled the Santa Fe Trail in 1821, blazing a way for traders and settlers to move west and turning Santa Fe into one of Mexico's most prosperous commercial centers. After the Mexican-American War, when New Mexico and California were ceded to the United States, Santa Fe continued in its role as the capital and commercial center of the new United States territory of New Mexico. With the 1880 arrival of the Atchinson, Topeka, and Santa Fe Railroad, Santa Fe experienced another economic and population boom, as travel and shipping to and from the city became a good deal easier and faster.

When New Mexico achieved statehood in 1912, Santa Fe was made the state capital and the number of visitors increased further—attracted by the city's climate, art, and culture as well as the art and culture of the Native American pueblos outside the city. Whether for business or personal reasons, visitors came to Santa Fe by the droves—sending home flocks of postcards that showcased Santa Fe's highlights: the Palace of the Governors, the oldest building in continuous use in the United States; the Oldest House in the United States; Tesuque, Pojoague, Nambe, San Ildefonso, San Juan, and Santa Clara Pueblos; and the beautiful "Santa Fe style" buildings found throughout the city.

Today, Santa Fe's unique blend of European, Native American, and Hispanic influences and culture continues to attract visitors from across the United States and around the world.

2004 TYPICAL MEXICAN HOME AND FAMILY

Greetings From
SANTA FE
NEW MEXICO

Colorful
SANTA FE
New Mexico

About Santa Fe

Historical Overview

The first inhabitants of the area that would become Santa Fe were Pueblo Indians, who lived in settlements scattered around the area. According to archaeologists, the sites were settled anywhere from 1050 to 1150 and abandoned approximately two hundred years before the arrival of the Spanish.

The first European settlement in Santa Fe was founded in 1607 by Spanish settlers under the leadership of Juan Martinez de Montoya. Three years later, Don Pedro de Peralta, Governor-General of the "Kingdom of New Mexico," moved the capital of New Mexico from San Juan Pueblo twenty-five miles south to Santa Fe—formally establishing a town there and making Santa Fe the second oldest city founded by Europeans in the United States. Don Pedro named the new town *La Villa Real de la Santa Fe de San Francisco de Asìs*, or "The Royal City of the Holy Faith of St. Francis of Assisi" in English.

The Spaniards ruled the region until 1680, when Native Americans from the pueblos around Santa Fe, under the leadership of a shaman priest named Popè, rose up against the Spanish government—killing four hundred settlers and driving the rest into Mexico. The victorious Pueblos burned and sacked most of Santa Fe, leaving only the Palace of Governors standing. The area reverted to Pueblo rule until 1692, when it was re-conquered by troops under the command of Don Diego de Vargas.

From 1692 to 1821, relations between the Spanish and the Pueblo People improved greatly, thanks in large part to a new Spanish policy of peaceful religious and civil coexistence and an alliance between the two groups against more hostile Native American groups like the Comanche, Apache, and Navajo.

In 1821, after Mexico gained its independence from Spain, Santa Fe became the capital of the Mexican province of New Mexico. This era also saw the end of the Spanish closed empire policy—a policy that severly limited trade between the Spanish and neighboring powers like the United States— and American traders and trappers were allowed to move into the region. Also in that year, William Becknell blazed the 1,000 mile route between Missouri and Santa Fe, becoming the first person to use the famous Santa Fe Trail. The trail later became a vital commercial and military route until the arrival of the railroad in 1880.

On August 18, 1846, during the United States' conflict with Mexico, Santa Fe was captured by American soldiers under the command of General Stephen Watts Kearny. Two years after this capture, the territories of New Mexico and California were ceded to the United States by Mexico in the Treaty of Guadalupe Hidalgo.

During the Civil War, Santa Fe changed hands again, coming under the administration of the Confederate States of America in March of 1862 as part of Confederate General Henry Hopkins Sibley's New Mexico Campaign. The campaign was largely unsuccessful and was stopped by Union forces at the Battle of Glorieta Pass.

Santa Fe reverted to Federal control, and after the Civil War it continued on as the capital of the Territory of New Mexico. With the coming of the telegraph in 1868 and the Atchinson, Topeka, and Santa Fe Railroad in 1880, Santa Fe prospered—undergoing an economic revolution and subsequent boom.

On January 6, 1912, New Mexico was admitted into the Union as the forty-seventh state, with Santa Fe as the state capital.

The Santa Fe Trail

From 1821 to 1880, the Santa Fe Trail was a major commercial and military highway leading from Missouri to New Mexico. First blazed by trader William Becknell, the Trail became a vital link between the American Southwest and the rest of the United States.

Beginning in Franklin, Missouri, the Trail crosses the Missouri River at Arrow Rock, passing north of Marshall, through Lexington and Fort Osage before ending up in Independence, the famous starting point for the Oregon and California Trails. After Independence, it continues on through Kansas, going through the towns of Olathe, Baldwin City, and Council Grove, then moves south to Lyons and the Arkansas River. Next, the Trail branches and follows both banks of the river upstream to Dodge City and Garden City. East of Garden City, the Trail branches even further. One of the branches follows the Arkansas River to the Colorado town of La Junta and from there heads to Watrous, New Mexico. The other goes through the Cimarron River Valley and Clayton, New Mexico, and then to Watrous. At Watrous, the two main branches join up and continue on to Santa Fe.

From 1821 to 1846, the Trail was the main commercial link between the United States and Mexico. In 1846, during the Mexican-American War, it was used by General Stephen Watt Kearney as an invasion route into Santa Fe. After the Mexican-American War, the Santa Fe Trail still served as an important connection between the United States and its new territories, with covered wagon trains arriving from all points east and a monthly stagecoach line running from Independence to Santa Fe.

In 1880, the Atchinson, Topeka, and Santa Fe Railroad brought a faster, safer, and more efficient means of travel to the Southwest, making the Santa Fe Trail obsolete. Today, the Santa Fe Trail is a historical attraction under the management of the National Park System.

The Hysterical Parade, Santa Fe. [Circa 1940s; $6-8]
From the back: "The Santa Fe Fiesta was instituted in 1712 by the Governor Marques de la Penuela to celebrate the re-conquest of the city and province by General DeVargas some sixteen years before. It is today one of the very oldest community celebrations in America. There is a historical pageant to celebrate the re-conquest. But the Hysterical Parade, a humorous affair lampooning almost everything imaginable, occurs on the last day of the Fiesta. The scene is, of course, the historical Santa Fe Plaza, the end of the Santa Fe Trail."

Starvation Peak on the Santa Fe Trail. [Circa 1920s; $3-4]
Legends abounded on the Santa Fe Trail and the story of Starvation Peak is no exception. The legend says that in the early days of Spanish exploration of the Southwest, a detachment of soldiers sought refuge from Native American attackers on this peak. They opted to die of starvation on the mountain rather than face death at the hands of their attackers.

[Circa 1940s; $2-3]

[Circa 1940s; $3-4]

Monument marking the end of the Santa Fe Trail. [Circa 1920s; $3-4]
The Santa Fe Trail began in Franklin, Missouri and was at the time the only highway connecting the Southwest to points east. The Trail was infamous for highway robberies, Indian attacks, lack of water, and other dangers.

The Pecos Ruins on the Santa Fe Trail. [Circa 1940s; $3-4]
From the back: "This ruined church and the ruins of a pueblo near which it stands are all that remain of what was for over 1000 years the largest town in what is now the United States. They are located on the Santa Fe trail, near Las Vegas. The Church was erected by the Franciscans about 1607. The old Pueblo of Cicuye immediately adjoining the Church was visited by Francisco Vasquez Coronado, in 1541, and by every other Spanish explorer in New Mexico in the sixteenth century. The Church and Pueblo were abandoned about 1883."

[Circa 1920s; $4-5]

Glorieta Pass, near the end of the Santa Fe Trail. [Circa 1940s; $4-5] The pass is well known as being the location of a decisive battle between Union and Confederate armies during the Civil War.

[Circa 1940s; $5-6]

Wagon Train. [Circa 1940s; $3-5]
Before railroad days, wagon trains such as this convoy of prairie schooners pulled by oxen made their way across rugged mountains and arid desert on the Santa Fe Trail. The journey was fraught with danger and it was a happy day indeed when travelers safely arrived in Santa Fe.

H-3509 OLD STAGE COACH RELAY STATION ON SANTA FE TRAIL, NEAR SANTA FE, NEW MEXICO.

Old Stagecoach relay station. [Circa 1920s; $5-6]
Until the coming of the railroad, the stagecoach was the foremost means of conveyance along the Santa Fe Trail. During the often perilous journey of twenty to twenty-five days, passengers frequently slept in relay stations such as these at intervals along the route.

End of the line. [Circa 1920s; $6-8]
The arrival of a stagecoach from the East was cause for great celebration for both passengers and townspeople. For passengers and crew, it meant they had safely arrived at their final destination; for residents of Santa Fe, it meant news and perhaps even mail from points east.

First train to Santa Fe. [Circa 1940s; $3-4]
A somewhat romantic view of the sighting by Native Americans of the first train into Santa Fe. It is based on a painting by Sauerwin.

The City of Santa Fe

The Palace of the Governors

The Palace of the Governors, located on the Plaza, was built in 1610 by Don Pedro de Peralta, who was also responsible for establishing Santa Fe as the capital of the Spanish "Kingdom of New Mexico." The Palace has been the seat of six separate governments as well as a museum and a public market, and consequently is the oldest occupied public building in the United States.

The original building was composed of a central palace along with a town hall, a gun powder magazine, an armory, a forge, a military chapel, at least four defensive towers, a granary, storerooms, warehouses, a carriage house, corrals, and several multipurpose sheds. After the 1680 Pueblo Revolt, the Palace, along with the rest of the city, was abandoned by the Spanish. When they returned in 1692, they found the Palace had been converted into more traditional pueblo-style apartments. Following Mexico's independence from Spain in 1821, the Palace of Governors became the seat of the Mexican government for the Province of New Mexico. In 1848, after New Mexico and California were ceded to the United States, the Palace became the seat of government for the United States Territory of New Mexico. Except for a very brief stint in Confederate hands, the Palace of the Governors was the official seat of government for the territory until a new state house was built in 1907.

Currently, it houses a branch of the Museum of New Mexico and an open air market specializing in handmade arts and crafts and operated by members of the Native American Vendors Program. The Palace of the Governors was designated as a Registered Historical Landmark in 1960 and an American Treasure in 1999.

Palace of the Governors. [Circa 1920s; $4-5]
Built in 1610, the Palace of the Governors was the seat of nearly three centuries of government and witness to a colorful history, including Spanish, Mexican, and American. For this reason, it is known as the oldest continuously occupied building in the United States.

Palace of the Governors [Circa 1940s; $3-4]
A brief history is related on the back of this card: "...built soon after the founding of the village of Santa Fe under the Spanish flag. Was abandoned during the Indiana Rebellion of 1680—reconquered by De Vargas in 1692 and remained under Spanish rule until the Independence of Mexico in 1821, continued under the Mexican flag until the American occupation of 1846. Under the confederate flag for two weeks during the Civil War, when it was retaken by the Federal Army. Here Gov. Lew Wallace wrote the latter part of *Ben Hur*. Was occupied by the various Governors until the building of the present State Capitol. It is now the Museum of the School of American Research."

[Circa 1940s; $5-6]

Palace of the Governors. [Circa 1920s; $5-6] This building was added to the National Register of Historic Places in 1966.

Palace of the Governors. [Circa 1950s; $5-6] The building was altered many times throughout its long history. This image shows the building with the addition of a portico. Known as "The Portal," or front porch, of the Palace of the Governors, it is reserved for the use of authorized participants in the Native American Vendors Program to display and sell wares they have made.

A more modern view of the Palace of the Governors, which now houses New Mexico's history museum. It was designated a Registered National Historic Landmark in 1960 and an American Treasure in 1999. [Circa 1950s; $2-3]

"Our Lady of Victory" celebration in front of the Palace of the Governors. [Circa 1950s; $6-7]

Palace of the Governors, Santa Fe. [Circa 1940s; $4-5]

Public Buildings

Santa Fe is home to a number of noteworthy public and government buildings—particularly the Palace of the Governors, which (as described in the previous section) has been home to six different governments and is the oldest occupied public building in the United States. The city is also home to the Roundhouse, which serves as the New Mexico State Capitol Building. Built in the shape of a Zia Pueblo symbolizing the sun and the Circle of Life, it is the only round capitol building in the United States. Due to rather strict building codes and architectural guidelines, the remainder of the public buildings (as well as many private residences) in Santa Fe are built in "Santa Fe Style," an architectural style that combines Spanish and Pueblo influences.

State Capitol Building, Santa Fe. [pre 1915; $5-6]
Completed in 1900 after a fire destroyed the previous capitol building, the new capitol was built at a cost of only $140,000.

[pre 1915; $4-5]

State Capitol Building, Santa Fe. [Circa 1940s; $3-4]
This is the building where President Taft signed the proclamation in 1912 admitting New Mexico to the Union.

[Circa 1940s; $3-4]

[Circa 1940s; $3-4]

[Circa 1940s; $3-4]
The dome was removed from the new capitol complex and the unified look is so-called "Territorial" style. It was a combination of Spanish and American design—and touted as the most unique capitol in the United States.

New New Mexico State Capitol, Santa Fe.
[Circa 1940s; $3-4]
Many additions and renovations were made on the state capitol throughout the years. In 1950, a major renovation project was begun to unify the look of the complex.

The *new, new* New Mexico State Capitol Building. [Circa 1950s; $1-2]
From the back: "completed and dedicated in December 1966, this new $5.2 million structure is probably the most unusual capitol building in the United States. Its circular shape has four entrances set to project the Zia Indian symbol of the sun. The elegant interior boasts fan-shaped legislative halls which open onto a 60-foot high rotunda. It was designed to retain some of the Spanish Colonial and Indian heritage of New Mexico."

Post Office and Government Building. [Circa 1920s; $3-4]
The unique architecture of this post office is known as "Santa Fe Style," and is constructed along the lines of southwest Pueblo Indian architecture distinctive to the Santa Fe area.

U.S. Post Office, Santa Fe. [Circa 1940s; $3-4]
Perhaps the most unusual post office building in the United States, the Santa Fe Post Office and Federal Building was located in the old part of the city.

The post office building is on the National Register of Historic Places. [Circa 1940s; $3-4]
It currently houses the Institute of American Indian Arts (IAIA) Museum.

[Circa 1940s; $3-4]

Supreme Court Building, Santa Fe. [Circa 1940s; $3-4]
Constructed in a style known variously as "New Mexico Territorial" or "New Mexico Colonial" style, the building was completed in 1937. Financing was partly with the help of PWA funds. This building was added to the National Register of Historic places in 2002.

U.S. Court House and Federal Building, Santa Fe. [pre 1915; $6-7]

Municipal Building, Santa Fe.
[Circa 1940s; $4-5]

Santa Fe train station. [$12]
Real-photo card of the D&RG/NMC Depot.

Ariel view of modern-day Santa Fe. [Circa 1940s; $4-5]

Art Museum of New Mexico, Santa Fe. [Circa 1940s; $4-5]
The Art Museum of New Mexico is the best example of "Mission Architecture" in Santa Fe. The building dates to 1617, making it 150 or so years *older* than the oldest missions in California.

H-3525 A STREET SCENE IN "OLD TOWN", SANTA FE, NEW MEXICO.

Old Town, Santa Fe. [Circa 1920s; $5-6]
From the back: "In Santa Fe, oldest city in the United States, it is difficult to say just where the so-called "Old Town" begins or leaves off..."

Art Museum of New Mexico. [Circa 1940s; $4-5]
The building was constructed as a monument to the Franciscan missionaries of the 17th and 18th centuries.

New Mexico Art Museum. [Circa 1940s; $3-4]

Art Museum Building, Santa Fe. [Circa 1940s; $3-4] From the back: "The building is used by the School of American Research as a treasure house of Southwestern art, beginning with the Indian of prehistoric times and coming down to the American artists of to-day [sic]."

The Governor's Mansion, Santa Fe. [Circa 1915; $6-7]
From the back: "This lovely mansion has been the home of various governors of New Mexico since the state was admitted into the Union in 1912. It replaced the old Palace of the Governors on the Plaza as their official residence."

[Circa 1940s; $3-4]

[Circa 1940s; $3-4]

Dahlia Gardens, Governor's Mansion. [Circa 1940s; $2-3]
The dahlia garden on the grounds of the mansion attracted visitors far and wide for the beauty and size of its flowers.

Sunken Garden and Lily Pool, Governor's Mansion. [Circa 1940s; $3-4]
The formality of the garden as well as the very atypical plantings made this garden an attraction to visitors.

St. Michael's College, Santa Fe. [Circa 1940s; $3-4] Now known as the College of Santa Fe, St. Michael's was opened in 1859 and was for a long time the only source of education for boys in the Territory of New Mexico.

SUNMOUNT SANITARIUM, SANTA FE, NEW MEXICO.

Sunmount Sanitarium, Santa Fe. [Circa 1920s; $4-5] From the back: "The dry climate of the Southwestern states is universally recognized as beneficial to those suffering from lung and throat trouble. Sunmount at Santa Fe, New Mexico, is one of the best known sanitariums in this part of the country."

The Plaza, Santa Fe, New Mexico. [Circa 1940s; $4-5]
The Plaza marked the end of the Santa Fe Trail, an oasis for road-weary travelers who made it to the end of the line. The Palace of the Governors is in the background.

Rebel Monument. [Circa 1940s; $3-4]
This monument, which was erected after the Civil War, is the only one in the United States referring to the Confederates as "Rebels."

Churches

When the Spanish came to New Mexico in the early 1600s, Franciscan missionaries traveled with them, anxious to convert the native population to Christianity. Among the legacies left behind by these missionaries were churches and missions scattered throughout New Mexico and in the pueblos around Santa Fe. During the Pueblo Revolt in 1680, a number of these missions were destroyed and the friars and missionaries who lived in them were killed or driven off. The missions that survive today still serve as places of worship, as well as being tourist attractions and examples of Mission style architecture.

San Miguel Church

Santa Fe is also home to the oldest church in the United States—the San Miguel Church, built in 1541. The upper walls of the church were destroyed in the Pueblo Revolt and rebuilt by Don Diego de Vargas when he re-conquered the territory in 1692.

San Miguel Church. [Circa 1915; $5-7]
The oldest church in the U.S. (Santa Fe also boasts the oldest cemetery and the oldest house). The cemetery can be seen to the left of the building in this early view.

San Miguel Church. [Circa 1915; $5-7]
This image shows the original design of San Miguel Church, the cradle of Christianity in the New Mexico Territory. Historians date the foundation of the church back to 1541.

[Circa 1915; $5-7]

San Miguel Church as it looked in 1872. [Circa 1915; $5-7] The upper portion of the tower fell during a storm in 1872 and was rebuilt in 1888. The walls are between three and five feet thick.

[Circa 1915; $6-8]

[Circa 1920; $6-7]

San Miguel Church. [Circa 1915; $6-8]
Many views exist to show the mission throughout it various renovations. It remains a top tourist destination and is visited by thousands of people every year.

OUR LADY OF GUADALUPE, SAN MIGUEL CHURCH, SANTA FE, NEW MEXICO.

Our Lady of Guadalupe, San Miguel Church. [Circa 1920; $5-6]
From the back: "This card represents the picture of Our Lady of Guadalupe, of miraculous origin, that was discovered on the 'tilma'—a long cloak used by Mexican Indians—of Juan Diego, an Indian shepherd, to whom Our Lady appeared in 1531, near Mexico City. This copy is over 300 hundred years old: the crown here shown was used only in the first copies of the original. An artist who made a special study of the pictures of Our Lady of Guadalupe declared that this is one of the best."

[Circa 1920s; $5-6]

[Circa 1940s; $4-5]

[Circa 1940s; $4-5]

[Circa 1940s; $3-5]

OLD BELL SAN JOSE, SAN MIGUEL CHURCH,
SANTA FE, NEW MEXICO

Old San Jose Bell, in San Miguel Church. [Circa 1940s; $3-5] From the back: "The old San Jose bell bearing the Spanish inscription 'San Jose ruega por nosotros'—St. Joseph, pray for us—was cast and hammered in Spain in 1356, brought to Santa Fe in 1712, and placed in the San Miguel Church in 1848. In is nearly four inches thick, about the size of the Liberty Bell and weighs 780 pounds. It is made of copper, silver, iron, and gold.

INTERIOR VIEW TOWARDS ENTRANCE, SAN MIGUEL CHURCH, SANTA FE, NEW MEXICO

Interior views, San Miguel Church. [Circa 1940s; $4-6] These two interior views of the church show the balcony, which is held up by carved beams that date back to the rebuilding of the church in 1710. On the walls are Spanish and Italian oil paintings depicting typical Christian scenes.

[Circa 1940s; $4-6]

INTERIOR OF SAN MIGUEL CHURCH, SANTA FE, NEW MEXICO. 118210

Other Historic Churches

Other area churches include the Saint Francis Cathedral, built by Archbishop Jean Baptiste Lamy; the Chapel of Our Lady of Light, location of the Miraculous Stairway; and the Christo Rey Church, the largest adobe structure in the Southwest.

Saint Francis Cathedral, Santa Fe. [Circa 1940s; $3-5]
Archbishop Jean Baptiste Lamy had the Cathedral built (see Bishop's Lodge). It was constructed around the structure know as La Parroquia and when it was completed in 1884, La Parroquia was torn down.

The Cathedral, Santa Fe. [Circa 1915; $5-7]
A small mission church originally stood where the cathedral now stands. It was burned during the Pueblo Revolt of 1680. In 1692, another, more substantial, adobe church was erected on the site. This building, known as La Parroquia, served for another two hundred years. Construction began on the current Cathedral, shown here, in 1869.

[Circa 1940s; $3-5]

The Cathedral of San Francisco de Assisi, Santa Fe. [Circa 1940s; $3-5]
The impressive stained-glass windows in the church were created n France, and transported to Santa Fe via ship and then overland via a covered wagon.

The Cathedral of San Francisco de Assisi, Santa Fe. [Circa 1940s; $3-5]
Under the Cathedral lie the remains of two Franciscan Friars who were killed by Indians in the 1680 uprising, as well as the remains of Archbishop Lamy.

The Academy and Chapel of Our Lady of Light, Santa Fe. [Circa 1940s; $3-5]
This impressive structure owes its existence to Jean Baptiste Lamy as well. Bishop Lamy took seriously his mission of bringing Catholicism and educational facilities to the New Mexico Territory. He asked the teaching order of the Sisters of Loretto to leave their homes in Kentucky and work with him to establish a girls' school in Santa Fe.

Our Lady of Light Chapel (Loretto), Santa Fe.
[Circa 1915; $6-7]
The Chapel was constructed in the Gothic Revival style patterned after Sainte-Chapelle in Paris; it must have made a striking contrast to the adobe churches previously seen in Santa Fe.

[Circa 1940s; $3-5]

SCOTTISH RITE CATHEDRAL, SANTA FE, NEW MEXICO.

Scottish Rite Cathedral, Santa Fe. [Circa 1940s; $3-5]
The Cathedral is almost an exact replica of the "Court of Lions" in the Alhambra in Granada, Spain. It is an imposing structure, situated on a slight rise above the city.

Miraculous Stairway, Loretto Chapel. [Circa 1940s; $3-5]
Legend states that upon completion of the chapel a century and a half ago, the Sisters of Loretto realized there was no way to gain access to the twenty-foot choir loft in the rear of the structure. The Sisters made a Novena (a prayer repeated for nine days) to Saint Joseph, patron saint of carpenters, with hopes of a solution. Legend has it that on the ninth day of the Novena, a white-bearded man, carrying his tool case and walking a donkey, arrived at the convent door looking for work. Over eight months, he created an ingenious spiral staircase composed of two 360-degree turns, absent a center post for support and lacking nails or wooden pegs to secure the structure. The identity of the miraculous carpenter was never known and he departed without seeking payment. The Chapel is now privately owned but continues to attract thousands of visitors a year; a small admission fee is charged to view the structure and "Miraculous Stairway."

[Circa 1915; $5-7]
The legend of the "Miraculous Stairway" was the subject of a recent made-for-TV movie, a much embellished telling of the tale, as well as a segment of *Unexplained Mysteries*.

El Cristo Rey Church, Santa Fe. [Circa 1940s; $3-5]
From the back: "Cristo Rey is the Catholic Church's Memorial to the Coronado Cuarto Centennial, 1940. The largest adobe structure in the Southwest, one hundred eighty thousand (4 x 10 x 18 inch) adobe bricks were used in the construction, being made on the site by natives. All native lumber was used, the enormous *vigas* (ceiling timbers), each weighing 2500 lbs., were hewn in the Chama mountain region. The weight of the Church is 15 million lbs."

Reredos, alter piece in el Cristo Rey, Santa Fe. [Circa 1940s; $3-5]
Cristo Rey was built around the artistic *Reredos* (alter piece), which many admit is the finest piece of stone sculpture in the U.S. from Spanish colonial times. The *Reredos* measures 18' x 32', is 32" thick, and weighs 450,000 lbs.

Presbyterian Church of Santa Fe. [Circa 1940s; $3-4] New Mexico was annexed in 1849 and the following year the first Presbyterian minister arrived in Santa Fe. However, the first real congregation of Presbyterians was not organized until 1867. The present church (shown), as well as several other buildings not shown, are all built in the Santa Fe Pueblo-Mission style of architecture. These buildings were dedicated in 1939.

The Santuario de Chimayo. [Circa 1940; $3-5] Located about thirty-five miles north of Santa Fe, *El Santuario de Chimayo* is an important tourist destination. From the back: "The fame of the healing powers of this historic shrine is world wide. It is said that the faith of the Santo Nino (Holy child) of Chimayo kept up the courage of many a prisoner thru the punishments of Bataan; and since coming home a large number of World War II veterans from New Mexico have made pilgrimages to Chimayo on foot without food or water to thank the Holy Child for their safe return."

Cross of the Martyrs, Santa Fe. [Circa 1940s; $3-4] From the back: "Erected by the Knights of Columbus and the Historical Society of New Mexico in memory of the Franciscan Friars who were killed by the Pueblo Indians in the Revolution of the Province of New Mexico Aug. 9th and 10th 1680."

RUINS OF ANCIENT SPANISH CEMETERY AND CHAPEL, SANTA FE, NEW MEXICO.

Chapel and cemetery ruins, Santa Fe. [Circa 1920s; $3-5] The ruins are some of the oldest in New Mexico, dating from the 17th century.

Cross of the Penitentes. [Circa 1940s; $3-4] From the back: "The Penitentes are a religious group found in the Spanish speaking communities of New Mexico. The full name of this society is Los Hermanos Penitentes del Tercer Orden de Franciscanos—and is a survival of Medieval times brought here by the early Spanish settlers. They have intense religious convictions and Pilgrimages from Calvary are made during Easter week. Outsiders are now permitted to witness parts of their ceremonies."

Oldest House

As the oldest capital city and the second oldest surviving city founded by Europeans in the United States, Santa Fe can lay claim to a number of landmark buildings. Besides the Palace of the Governors and the San Miguel Church, these buildings include the Oldest House in the United States.

According to some, the house was standing when conquistador Francisco Vasquez de Coronado made his expedition into New Mexico searching for the fabled golden city of Cibola. Whether or not this is true, it has been proven that the house dates back to at least 1598, when Spanish settlers were first coming into New Mexico. Today, the house is not a private residence but is maintained as a historic landmark and tourist attraction.

Oldest House, Santa Fe. [pre 1915; $6-7]
From the back: "An old adobe structure situated in the heart of the oldest district of Santa Fe, New Mexico, seems to have a well supported claim to distinction as the oldest house in the Unites States. It is claimed that this house was standing when Coronado discovered a native village upon the present site of Santa Fe in 1540, forty-five years before the settlement of St. Augustine, Florida—and it is known to have at least dated from the foundation of the Spanish City in 1598. Of late years the house has deteriorated, but every effort is being made to preserve it."

Oldest House in the U.S., Santa Fe. [Circa 1930s; $4-6]
One may get the feeling that everything is Santa Fe is old—this house is no exception, having been given the title of "oldest house in the U.S." The structure is said to have been part of the original ancient Indian pueblo of *Tiguex,* and dates to at least 1598.

[Circa 1920s; $5-6]

THE OLDEST HOUSE IN AMERICA, SANTA FE, NEW MEXICO.

[pre 1915; $5-6]

THE OLDEST HOUSE IN AMERICA, SANTA FE, NEW MEXICO.

Both pages:
Oldest House, Santa Fe. [Circa 1915; $5-7] Originally a two story structure, the home's top level was reached by ladders through openings in the first level ceiling. The building is much deteriorated, as these images confirm.

[pre 1920; $5-6]

[Circa 1940s; $3-4]

[Circa 1940s; $3-4]

Both pages:
Oldest House in America, Santa Fe.
These much romanticized views of the oldest house in the U.S. show the building with its two stories intact. One card relates that "according to tradition, the Oldest House was the residence of an Indian Chief in the Pueblo of 'Cua-Pooge'—(mussel-pearl-place-on-the-water); neither the Spaniards nor the Tlascala Indians, who came from Mexico, built two-story adobe houses."

[Circa 1940s; $2-3]

Rear view of the oldest house. [Circa 1940s; $3-4]
From the back: "The niche in the lower part of the rear outside wall was used by the Indians as a place of storage. Originally, this wall formed part of another room that has been destroyed. This picture also shows the Indian community oven where bread was baked and meat stewed."

Staying in Santa Fe

La Fonda

Literally located at the end of the Santa Fe Trail, the La Fonda (in Spanish "The Boardinghouse") has been a Santa Fe landmark since the early nineteenth century and is one of Santa Fe's most famous hostelries. Back in 1607, when the area was first settled by Europeans, an inn was one of the first businesses established in the new settlement. It continued to provide meals and rooms throughout the era of Spanish rule. When William Becknell and his party arrived in Santa Fe in 1821, they were pleased to find food and lodging waiting for them right on the edge of the Plaza. From that point on, the La Fonda became connected with the history of the Santa Fe Trail—when tired and dusty travelers finally reached Santa Fe, there was the La Fonda with its doors open, offering food, drink, and a place to spend the night.

Even after the Santa Fe Trail became obsolete, the La Fonda still attracted guests, becoming one of Santa Fe's premier hotels and hosting such notables as Salvador Dali, Zsa Zsa Gabor, and Presidents Ulysses S. Grant and Rutherford B. Hayes and their wives. By 1920, the hotel was very old and in fairly poor shape, so the building was razed, rebuilt, and then purchased by the Atchinson, Topeka, and Santa Fe Railroad. Since 1968, it has been locally owned and operated.

ANCIENT LA FONDA WHICH STOOD ON SITE OF PRESENT HOTEL, SANTA FE, NEW MEXICO.

32553

La Fonda, Santa Fe.
[Circa 1940s; $3-4]
From the back: "For generations this ancient hostelry stood in Santa Fe, New Mexico, at the end of the Santa Fe Trail. Here it was that the old stagecoaches and traders' caravans halted after the arduous and dangerous journey across mountain and prairie from 'The States.' It was the rendezvous of celebrities, pioneers, traders, gamblers, and adventurers in the 'early days.' With the coming of the railroad and the disuse of 'The Trail,' La Fonda fell into decay and ruin, but when the automobiles in ever increasing numbers revived the historic Santa Fe Trail, a beautiful modern hostelry was erected on this site."

The present edifice of La Fonda. [Circa 1920s; $5-6]
After much of the ancient building of La Fonda was abandoned and burned, the residents of Santa Fe raised almost a quarter of a million dollars by public subscription, with which to rebuild this historic building.

The modern La Fonda, Santa Fe. [Circa 1940s; $4-5]

Interior views of La Fonda, Santa Fe. [Circa 1940s; $7-8]
These interior views show the unique, colorful combination of American Indian, Mexican, and New Mexican history embodied in the atmosphere of this historic Inn.

[Circa 1940s; $7-8]

[Circa 1940s; $7-8]

[Circa 1940s; $7-8]

Courtyard, La Fonda, Santa Fe. [Circa 1940s; $7-8]
The rough-flagged patio (or *placita*) surrounding a traditional fountain welcomes guests from all over the world.

[Circa 1940s; $6-7]

[Circa 1940s; $5-6]

Patio Entrance, La Fonda. [Circa 1940s; $5-6]
From the back: "This lovely entrance from San Francisco St. into La Fonda ha been the motif for several successful etchings and painting by eminent artists. Looking across the quiet Patio the ancient Spanish Cathedral of St. Francis may be seen in the background."

South Portal Lounge, La Fonda. [Circa 1940s; $7-8]
Afternoon tea being served in the lounge—the large fireplace on the right warms the entire room on cool winter days.

The Bishop's Lodge

In 1851, Jean Baptiste Lamy arrived in Santa Fe from southern Ohio, where he had been doing mission work. He was responsible for establishing the first school for teaching English in Santa Fe and for helping to establish several other schools as well. He was made bishop in 1853 and archbishop in 1875. To escape the pressures and frustrations of religious politics in Santa Fe, Archbishop Lamy built a small retreat in the foothills of the Sangre de Cristo Mountains, four miles outside the city.

In 1912, the lodge was purchased by Denver mining executive James R. Thorpe from the Pulitzer family. In 1998, it was purchased by an Australian real estate company and completely refurbished.

The Bishop's Lodge Chapel. [Circa 1950s; $6-7]
Lamy built the chapel as part of his private retreat; it is a popular destination for wedding ceremonies to this day. The story of the bishop is the subject of a popular novel by Willa Cather, *Death Comes for the Archbishop*. Today, the chapel is listed on the National Register of Historic Places.

The Bishop's Lodge, Santa Fe. [Circa 1940s; $5-6]
Named for the first bishop of Santa Fe, Jean Baptiste Lamy. The Bishop's Lodge is located four miles north of Santa Fe, in the foothills of the Sangre de Cristo mountain range.

The Bishop's Lodge. [Circa 1920s; $6-7] Lamy was well-known for his hospitality, and an invitation to the lodge was a high honor indeed. Today, it is one of the premier resorts and spas in New Mexico.

[Circa 1930s; $5-7]

[Circa 1940s; $5-6]

Other Hotels

Besides the historic La Fonda and the picturesque Bishop's Lodge, Santa Fe is home to a number of additional hotels and inns, all catering to the city's thriving tourist trade. Hotels like the Hotel de Vargas, the Galiesto, and the El Ortiz were built to house the growing number of visitors that followed the arrival of the railroad and the advent of the automobile.

Hotel De Vargas, Santa Fe. [Circa 1920s; $7-9] This early, though somewhat damaged, postcard view of the De Vargas Hotel shows an imposing Victorian structure that sadly burned to the ground—rather mysteriously, it is rumored—in January 1922. Stories abound regarding the cause of the fire, but most center on a mysterious explosion from the basement area, where a permanent guest, frustrated with Prohibition, was said to have installed a copper still to produce peach brandy.

New Hotel De Vargas, Santa Fe. [Circa 1940s; $4-6] The new Hotel De Vargas was reconstructed with the insurance money, at a location on Don Gaspar Street. The style was reminiscent of the Early California Mission Revival, more in keeping with the surrounding architecture of the time.

Hotel De Vargas. [Circa 1940s; $6-8] The hotel was entirely refurbished in 1986, and reopened under new proprietorship as the St. Francis Hotel. It is one of the finest in Santa Fe.

Galisteo Motel, Santa Fe. [Circa 1940s; $5-6]
Still within walking distance of the Plaza, the Galisteo is located in a quiet area outside the flow of traffic.

La Posada Inn, Santa Fe. [Circa 1960s; $1-2] From the back: "This beautiful outdoor fire-place in the central patio of La Posada adds to the touch of gracious living in the City Different at the end of the Santa Fe Trail."

El Ortiz, New Santa Fe Hotel. [pre 1915; $5-7]
El Oritz was built by the Santa Fe Railroad of adobe in a style of architecture similar to New Mexico buildings of the early 1800s.

Native Americans

Cave Dwellings

More than a million years ago, the Jemez Caldera, a massive volcano near the area that would become Santa Fe, erupted with titanic force—spewing out tons of lava and ash and forming the Jemez Mountains. Wind, rain, and snow gradually eroded the surface of the mountains, creating a series of sheer cliffs, a rather hard surface covering the soft volcanic tuff, and a multitude of caves in the cliffs. These caves and others around the Southwest would eventually become the homes for a prehistoric society of Native Americans who were the ancestors of several modern tribes.

Long before Europeans even considered traveling to the New World, a mysterious society of Native Americans dwelled among the cliffs and caves of the Southwest. These ancestral Puebloans, or Anasazi as they are also known, are best known for the unique style of their pottery and the sandstone, adobe, and jacal dwellings they left behind. The most well-preserved of these dwellings can be found in National Parks like Chaco Culture National Historical Park, Mesa Verde National Park, and Bandelier National Monument near Santa Fe. There, visitors can hike through Frijoles Canyon and see a number of restored kivas and dwellings built on the canyon floors, constructed in hollowed caves on the canyon walls, or built against the canyon walls. Also near Santa Fe was the Puye Pueblo, a large network of communal buildings and cliff dwellings located on the Pajarito Plateau.

Ancient cliff dwellings, near Santa Fe. [Circa 1920; $3-6] From the back: "This cliff dwelling contains about three hundred rooms cut in the stone. The entrance shown, leads to ten different room's ranging in size from 18 x 14 feet and upwards."

PREHISTORIC PUEBLO IN FRIJOLES CANYON, NEW MEXICO. 81340

Prehistoric pueblo in Frijoles Canyon, near Santa Fe. [Circa 1920s; $3-5] Frijoles Canyon contains many prehistoric ruins that include the community house called Tyuonyi and Ceremonial Cave. The canyon includes a designated wilderness area of 32,737.2 acres.

H-1582 CLIFF RUINS, RITO DE LOS FRIJOLES, NEAR SANTA FE, NEW MEXICO

[Circa 1940s; $2-3]

North wall ruins, Frijoles Canyon. [Circa 1940s; $3-4]
From the back: "These ancient ruins extend about two miles along Frijoles Canyon. The houses were built against the perpendicular wall. The large caves were excavations made for back rooms of the houses, the round holes being carved out for poles for [access to] roofs and ceilings—in some instances parts of the *vigas* remain."

Pueblo of Puye, near Santa Fe. [Circa 1915; $2-3]
It is believed that the Puye Pueblo was first inhabited in the late 1100s and abandoned about 1580 when a prolonged drought made it impossible to farm the area. Approximately 1,440 people once lived here.

Cliff dwellings, Puye Pueblo, near Santa Fe. [Circa 1940s; $2-4]
From the back: "The Kiva is the center of all religious and ceremonial life among the ancient cliff dwellers as it is among their descendants, the Pueblo Indians of today. It was and is a large turret-shaped building, mostly underground. Entrance is through a hatch in the roof, a long ladder, made from tall saplings being used to descend into it."

Excavated type of cliff dwellings in the Puye ruins near Santa Fe. [Circa 1940s; $3-5]
The word Pu-ye means "the assembling place of cottontail rabbits." The Puye Cliff Dwellings is a National Landmark and is owned and operated as a cultural monument by the pueblo of Santa Clara.

Prehistoric cave dwellings, Pueblo of Puye. [Circa 1940s; $2-4]
From the back: "Once in the long ago, Puye was the center of a dense population on the Pajarito plateau. Most of these 'ancients' lived in huge communal dwellings. Others occupied caves in the cliffs. Little is left today but memories."

Stone tents, Santa Clara Pueblo, near Santa Fe. [pre 1915; $4-5]
From the back: "Here in New Mexico are monuments of an ancient people; mute evidence of a race of long ago. These mysterious cliff dwellings, like swallows' nests, mark the faces of the canyon walls for hundreds of miles in Northern New Mexico."

Pueblos

When the Spanish came to the New Mexico territory, they found groups of Native Americans dwelling in villages comprised of buildings made from adobe and timber. They called these villages and the people that lived in them "pueblos," which is Spanish for town. These towns were made up of both individual structures and community buildings, frequently located in easily defensible locations and relying on trade and agriculture for subsistence. Religious life centered around the kiva, where private religious ceremonies were conducted.

There are currently twenty-five pueblos located in the Southwest. Nineteen of these are in New Mexico and six are located within thirty miles of Santa Fe. The pueblos around Santa Fe are Tesuque, Pojoague, Nambe, San Ildefonso, San Juan, and Santa Clara Pueblos.

Known throughout the Southwest for their beautiful artwork and fascinating culture, a number of New Mexican pueblos are listed on the National Register of Historic Places.

Taos Pueblo structures. [Circa 1930s; $10-12] Said to have been constructed between 1300 and 1450 A.D., the pueblo structures—including the communal dwellings shown here—are made entirely of adobe, earth mixed with straw and water. One structure is seven stories high and the other is five stories high.

Taos North House. [Circa 1930s; $5-7] The structures known as the North House or *Hlauuma*, are said to be the oldest continually inhabited structures in the United States. About 150 people reside full-time in the North and South Houses with the Pueblo.

Taos Pueblo. [Circa 1940s; $4-6]
From the back: "This is one of the oldest and most famous of all the Indian Pueblos. Long before the white man dreamed of land beyond the Atlantic, the Indians built "skyscrapers" of which Taos is the best surviving example. The Indians are stalwart, very conservative and little effected by contact with white man. Nearby is the town of Taos, home and burial place of Kit Carson, and seat of the famous Taos Art Colony."

Taos Pueblo. [Circa 1940s; $4-6]
Today, residents of the pueblo live much as their ancestors did, without electricity or running water. Tourists are welcomed into the pueblo only during specified hours and for special public ceremonies. The pueblo is closed to the public during some tribal events.

[Circa 1915; $7-9]

Taos Pueblo. [Circa 1950s; $1-3] One of the most picturesque scenes in all of New Mexico is the Taos Pueblo, set against the stunning backdrop of the Sangre de Cristo Mountains. From the back: "Brown dirt paths, hard trodden through the centuries, hug the foundations of the pueblos…"

Hotel Don Fernando, Taos. [Circa 1920s; $7-8] A once-prominent structure in the town of Taos, this image of the Hotel Don Fernando clearly shows the *vigas* that support heave adobe walls and clay-tiled roofs.

Hotel Don Fernando,
Taos. [Circa 1920s; $6-8]

The Plaza, Taos. [Circa 1940s; $4-5]
From the back: "Here are held the *fiestas* and many a courtship according to the ancient Spanish custom was born here *[sic]*. Trappers, miners, traders, and adventurers of the early American occupation told stories of their experiences. In more recent years it was a picturesque setting for local artists."

Ruins of an old Indian mission, Taos. [Circa 1940s; $3-4] The mission of San Geronimo (St. Jerome) was built by the Franciscan Friars in 1635. It had been in continuous use until it was destroyed in 1847 during the Taos Indian Uprising and massacre.

[1915; $8-10]

[Circa 1940s; $3-4]

The Indians of Taos Pueblo.
To anyone seeing Taos Pueblo for the first time, the words on the back of the card must truly describe their feelings: "A land utterly alien and astonishing. The superb Taos Indians still rove the country north of their pueblo, independent both of other peoples and their possessions. The old traditions and religious customs so arrogant, so proud, so magnificently are they clung to, that the pueblo dwellers merit a place among the great peoples of the world."

[1915; $5-7]

Taos Indian.
A distinguishing feature of the Taos Indian is his everyday dress of white robe in summer and red or blue blanket in winter.

[Circa 1915; $6-7]

[Circa 1940s; $3-4]

[Circa 1930s; $6-7]

[Circa 1930s; $6-7]

White-robed Taos Indian.
From the back: "This picturesque everyday dress of the Taos Indians strengthens their resemblance to the Arab. In winter a blanket replaces the sheet. The many bee-hive shaped ovens are used constantly for baking bread and other food."

[Circa 1940s; $3-4]

Taos Pueblo Indian. [Circa 1915; $6-8]

Santa Clara Indian Pueblo. [Circa 1940s; $3-4] From the back: "This pueblo whose Indian name Kha-Po, has the poetic meaning 'where roses bloom near the water,' is located on the Rio Grande about 30 miles north of Santa Fe. The inhabitants numbering about 300 belong the Tewa Tribe. The pueblo is famed for the beautiful black pottery made by the women."

Water Carrier, Taos. [Circa 1915; $6-8] Romantic view of Native American water carrier at Taos Pueblo.

Old church at Rancho de Taos. [Circa 1940s; $3-4] From the back: "One of the finest specimens still standing of the early New Mexican architecture. It is massively constructed of adobe with two towers in front, the upper portions built of wood, and each surmounted by a cross. The main body measures 108 feet inside. *Vigas* are sustained by carved supports imbedded in the walls, and any *vigas* are also carved. According to the best knowledge, the church was built in 1772, and many objects of great interest remain unchanged."

Taos Mission Church. [Circa 1940s; $3-4] Formally called the Saint Francis of Assisi Church at Rancho de Taos, Taos Mission Church is a formidable adobe structure and considered one of the most painted and photographed buildings in the United States. It was painted on multiple occasions by Georgia O'Keefe and photographed by Ansel Adams and Paul Strand.

Old Mission Church, Rancho de Taos. [Circa 1940s; $3-4] The Spanish Colonial adobe building has twin bell towers and an arched portal entrance that overlooks an enclosed courtyard. The church has a long history of serving the peoples of Taos, whatever their religious affiliation. It has been burned, destroyed, and rebuilt many times throughout its long history. In fact, each year after the rainy season, the church is "rebuilt" anew by an army of volunteers who re-apply a fresh layer of adobe to every exterior surface. The mission is an active parish and a National Historic Landmark.

Tesuque Indian Pueblo. [Circa 1940s; $3-4] From the back: "The Pueblo nearest to Santa Fe, the name meaning 'cottonwood Tree Place.' The Tesuques are a branch of the Tewas, and altho [sic] a small tribe are well known for their distinctive Raingods, drums and paintings."

Dances and Ceremonies

The Native American pueblos that existed in the Santa Fe area long before the arrival of Europeans each had their own language, culture, and ways of doing things. Part of this culture—the part that seems to be most fascinating to non-natives—includes the elaborate dances and ceremonies held throughout the year.

These dances and ceremonies are most often conducted over a period of several days and involve elaborate preparations, secret ceremonies, and public dances and pantomimes. Some are performed in secret in the confines of homes and kivas and are only witnessed by the participants or members of a certain clan or society. Others are performed in public and outsiders are allowed to watch. They take place for a variety of reasons, often having some kind of religious significance and performed or observed in conjunction with a particular event or for a particular time of year. In the pueblos, for example, a large public dance is performed in honor of the pueblo's patron saint on that particular saint's feast day. Dances like these usually included a Christian mass and procession along with a more traditional dance.

Ceremonial dress, Santa Fe. [Circa 1940s; $6-8]
From the back: "Picturesque and colorful, the costumes of the Native Americans of New Mexico helps to preserve the way of the ancients. The children are taught from a young age the rituals of their ancestors."

Ceremonial dances. [Circa 1940s; $5-8] Two of the most colorful dances performed by Native Americans throughout the year are the corn dance and the hoop dance. The corn dance involves both men and women in an elaborate dance depicting the planting of corn at the beginning of the growing season.

Taos Indian boys singing to their sweethearts. [Circa 1940s; $5-7]
This image was taken from a mural painted by J.R. Willis. From the back: "Following a good old ancient custom, the Taos Indian boys congregate on the bridge which separates the two villages on moonlight nights, play their flutes and sing to their sweethearts who line up on the opposite shore in appreciation of the entertainment."

[Circa 1940s; $5-7]

[Circa 1920s; $6-8]

Fiesta of San Geronimo, Taos Pueblo.
Held annually at the end of September, the Fiesta of San Geronimo is cause for great celebration among the residents of Taos Pueblo. A foot race is held between the pueblos to the north and those to the south. Tourists may attend the festival, keeping in mind that it is a religious celebration.

[1915; $7-9]

St. Geronimo Day, Taos Pueblo. [pre 1915; $6-8]
A rather crudely hand colored card. From the back: "The buildings of New Mexico villages are made of adobe and are quaint and interesting to travelers. This picture was taken on a holiday, September 30, and shows the procession leaving the church.

Pottery, Weaving, and Silver

The pottery, silver jewelry, and rugs made by Pueblo, Apache, and Navajo craftsmen are other aspects of Native American culture that have been popular with visitors to Santa Fe.

The Pueblo tradition of making pottery began prior to the arrival of the Europeans in the early 1600s. Since the concept of a pottery wheel was unknown to the Pueblo people, the pottery was made by hand without any mechanical assistance. Coils of clay were rolled and then wound into a pot shape. The potter would scrape the sides with her fingers or a shard of pottery to smooth the clay and draw it up towards the top. Thin strips of colored clay were then wiped on the surface. After the pot had dried, it was polished with a smooth stone, hand-painted, and fired in an open pit.

The art of weaving was introduced to the Navajo by the Pueblos, who had been growing cotton and weaving the fibers since the 800s. With the Spanish introduction of sheep, the Navajo began using wool instead of cotton fibers; by the 1800s, they were using wool exclusively. Like the Pueblo pottery, Navajo rugs and blankets were made without mechanical assistance, with the wool being carded, spun, dyed, and woven completely by hand. The Navajo also learned silversmithing from the Pueblos, who had been taught this craft by the Spanish.

As the popularity of these handmade items became more and more popular with collectors and museums, Santa Fe became a center for Native American art and artists and is now home to a number of dealers and galleries specializing in Native American ceramic and textile art plus silver jewelry.

Chimayo weaver. [Circa 1940s; $5-7] Weavers from Chimayo, like this one using an elaborate loom, are famous for their intricate geometric designs.

Pottery makers. [Circa 1940s; $6-8] These pottery makers are from the San Ildefonso Pueblo near Santa Fe. San Ildefonso is best known as the birthplace of the world-renowned black-on-black pottery with black matte designs developed by María Martínez along with her husband, Julian. Some of this pottery is shown in the foreground of this image.

Navajo rug weavers. [Circa 1940s; $6-8] More Native American rug weavers, this time Navajo, showing all stages of rug-making from carding the wool, making thread, and weaving the fantastic geometric designs.

Indian jewelry makers. [Circa 1940s; $6-8]
Three steps to traditional jewelry-making are shown—setting stones (turquoise), stamping designs on the pieces, and hammering the silver into shape.

The silversmith's daughter. [Circa 1940s; $4-6]
This charming pose is of a young Indian girl in traditional costume lavished with turquoise jewelry that is typical of the Navajo regions of New Mexico. The little girl wears not only multiple beaded necklaces and bracelets, but also rings and earrings.

Desert Life

[Circa 1940s; $1-2]

[Circa 1940s; $2-3]

[Circa 1940s; $1-2]

[Circa 1940s; $1-2]

Chiles

A part of the human diet since 7500 BC, the chile pepper (in New Mexico, the Spanish spelling of chili is used) was one of the first crops cultivated in the Americas. The chile was introduced to Europe by Diego Alvarez Chanca, a physician who traveled with Columbus on his second voyage to the Caribbean. These new plants were named peppers because they tasted similar to the kinds of peppers found in Europe. From there, they spread around the world, their spicy taste quickly becoming part of local cuisines.

In the Southwest, where the climate is ideally suited for the growing and drying of these peppers, the chile is a part of the indispensable trinity of chile, corn, and beans. Chopped and mixed into sauces and salsas, dried and crushed into powder, stuffed, roasted, or fried, the chile is integral as an ingredient or garnish for a multitude of Southwestern dishes.

The chile is so popular in New Mexico that *ristras*, strings of dried chiles, are sold as decorations and can be found hanging from the eaves of many a Santa Fe home.

Images of chilis (red peppers) drying in the sun, Santa Fe. [Circa 1915; $3-5]
A nearly ubiquitous sight in this area, nothing says New Mexico like red pepper *ristras* drying in the sun. The hot, dry climate is ideal for drying the chili, New Mexico's largest agricultural crop.

[Circa 1940s; $1-2]

From the back: "Nowhere can any landscape be found more colorful than that of New Mexico during the Indian summer, with its aspens turning to gold, with its fruit bearing trees turning red and orange and above all with the scarlet chili drying on the roof of the houses." [Circa 1920s; $3-5]

[Circa 1920s; $3-5]

Red chilis adorn an ancient mud *jacal*. [Circa 1940s; $2-4]
Chile peppers have been grown in New Mexico for thousands of years; without a doubt, New Mexicans consume more chilis per capita than in any other state.

Picturesque Southwest architecture. [Circa 1940s; $2-4]
From the back: "...you cannot help but observe the influence of the beautiful simplicity of the old Colonial Spanish settlers, associated with the care-free existence of these descendants of the Spanish *Conquistadores*. The beautiful hollyhocks and abundance of Chili drying upon the walls during the fall, present a colorful atmosphere, found only in the Southwest."

Burros

Like the chile, the burro is a symbol of the history, character, and culture of Santa Fe, New Mexico, and the Southwest. The domestication of the donkey can be traced back to ancient Egypt, where they were used as riding mounts and beasts of burden. The Southwestern burro (Spanish for donkey) is a descendent of the animals brought by Spanish explorers and settlers and from animals used and abandoned by prospectors. Like the mustang, some herds of burros that run wild are descendents of animals that escaped or were abandoned.

Longer-lived and cheaper to maintain than horses—and with greater agility and endurance on the narrow rocky trails found throughout the Southwest—burros were perfect for farmers or prospectors who lived high in the mountains or in the desert and could not afford a horse. They would frequently accompany traders on trips along the Santa Fe Trail.

Although cars and trucks have long since replaced the burro as convenient modes of transportation, burros are still frequently kept as pets or run wild in the mountains and deserts of the Southwest.

Burros, near Santa Fe.
[pre 1920; $3-5]
Throughout history, the burro has maintained a place of honor as part pack animal, part family member. From the back: "Even in the present day when factories produce farm wagons and other equipment that can be bought by almost anyone, the Mexican still clings tenaciously to the method of transportation used long ago by his fathers. He does not know, nor does he care, whether they lived in a mountainous region where only burros could traverse the trails, or whether they lived where wagons could be used and were too poor to obtain them. The one thing he does know is that his father used burros, and he cares for nothing better or more modern."

Burros loaded with alfalfa. [Circa 1915; $6-7]
Originally from Africa (where they were called wild asses), the burros of the American Southwest deserts have survived due to their unique ability to withstand the dry, arid conditions to which they are subjected. The burros that once were domesticated and used as pack and farm animals are now considered wild. Efforts have been made in recent years to stem their population as their numbers increase. There are many programs available for the adoption of these beautiful creatures.

Going to town. [Circa 1940s; $4-6]
Burros, which are not native to the United States, were brought in by early Spanish explorers in the 1500s as beasts of burden. Burros are sure on their feet and able to carry an enormous load compared to their size. They are normally patient, obedient animals.

Indian rider. [Circa 1940s; $3-5]
A means of transportation as well as a pack animal, the burro is the faithful companion of anyone who ventures out into the Southwest desert.

[Circa 1940s; $2-4]

[Circa 1940s; $2-3]

Baby burros. What could be cuter than baby burros with their mothers? These cards offer a much romanticized view of these animals, however. In reality, burros were used heavily as beasts of burden, for transportation, and occasionally, for food.

[Circa 1940s; $1-3]

Burro, New Mexico. [Circa 1940s; $1-3]
A whimsical view of New Mexico's beast of burden. Front verse: *O, don't you remember the desert, old pal, the desert with scenery like this. A Joshua Palm and a lonesome old jack, the fortune you dream of but miss.*

Threshing wheat with goats. [Circa 1920s ; $5-7]
Another beast of burden, the goat was used, among other things, for threshing wheat. They would be driven by dogs to trample the just-harvested wheat. After a time, they were driven off, the straw piled to one side, and the wheat gathered.

Cowboys

Perhaps one of the most widely known symbols of the Southwest is the cowboy. Popularized in almost every media imaginable, the hard-bitten, range-riding lone "cowpoke" has become an iconic representation of the toughness, hardiness, and strength of the Southwest, and of the United States in general.

The first cowboy traditions came to America in the sixteenth century from Spain. As the Spanish settled throughout Mexico and the surrounding territory, the traditions and culture of the *vaqueros* (Spanish for "cattle tender") spread as well. After winning its independence from Spain in 1821, Mexico opened its borders to American settlers. As these settlers moved in, some of them were absorbed into the existing *vaquero* culture, adopting the attire and vocabulary of the Mexican cowboys. In the California territory, a similar *vaquero* tradition had also developed and, after the Civil War, traveled west, mixing with the Mexican tradition. In time, cowboys began developing their own distinct culture, some of which is still evident today.

As part of New Mexico, Santa Fe has long been home to the *vaquero*—and later cowboy—culture, and the large number of ranches around the city have kept the culture alive and thriving to this day. Though fences have made free range cattle driving impossible, and trains and trucks make long cattle drives impractical and impossible, cowboys are still a part of Santa Fe's culture and population.

Cowboys of the Southwest. [Circa 1940s; $4-6]

Cowboys in the desert. [Circa 1920s; $5-7]
Cowboys in the desert faced a unique hardship when traveling on horseback. Not only did they need to provide enough water for themselves, but also for their mounts, as drinking holes could be scarce.

Cowboy of the old Southwest. [Circa 1940s; $3-5]
From the back: "A picturesque sight of ancient times frequently seen in the 'Ole Southwest and Mexico.' Here is shown the modern and ancient beasts of burden, the donkey, still used to carry water and food."

Breaking camp, New Mexico. [Circa 1940s; $6-8]
This rather elaborate camp set-up includes multiple cooking pots as well as shelves for additional cookware and supplies.

Calf roping on the open range. [Circa 1940s; $3-5]

Rock Formations and Mountain Passes

Twenty-seven million years ago, major fault lines running from Colorado to New Mexico pushed up sheets of rock, creating the Sangre de Cristo Mountain range—so named by Spanish explorers because of the red color the rocks take on at sunrise and sunset. In addition, as noted earlier, the huge volcano known as Jemez Caldera erupted over one million years ago near the area that would become Santa Fe, forming, among other things, the Jemez Mountains.

Over thousands of years, other tectonic upheavals—combined with erosion caused by wind, rain, and snow—sculpted those mountains and other rock formations into all manner of fantastic shapes, creating geological oddities like Camel and Monument Rocks located near Santa Fe. Other forces of nature, such as the Rio Grande River, also contributed to the shape of the landscape—carving out many canyons and valleys in the mountains around Santa Fe.

Santa Fe, Taos Highway, US Route 64. [Circa 1940s; $1-3]
From the back: "In the days of the pioneers, travelers journeyed from Santa Fe to Taos in ox-carts and stage coaches over the dangerous, narrow road throughout the gorge of the Rio Grande with its precipitous walls. Today, this fine modern highway follows a route of scenic and diversified beauty. For miles it follows the course of the Rio Grande leaving the river to wind through the mountains to the plateau surrounding Taos—artist's paradise and home of the famed Taos Indians."

Taos Hill, US Route 64. [Circa 1940s; $1-3] Although it does not look possible due to the narrowness of the roadway, the information on the back of the card suggests that one halt often to take in the beauty of the mountains and the flora of the canyons as they dip into the Rio Grande.

La Bajada Hill, near Santa Fe. [Circa 1920s; $2-4] Spanish for "the drop" or "the descent," *La Bajada* Hill is so named because it is a drop of about one thousand feet from the rim of the mesa to the lowland at the bottom. It accomplishes this by a series of twenty-three cut-backs or "hair-pin" turns through the one and a half mile long descent. The road is perfectly safe (so says the information on the back of the card!) because the roadway has been widened at each turn to accommodate even the largest automobile. Those turns deemed most dangerous have stone retaining walls to keep cars from going off the road and down the cliff.

Along the upper Rio Grande on the road to Taos. [pre 1915; $3-4]
From the back: "The country is one of startling contrasts. Each turn in the road presents some new combination of eroded hills and cliffs, belts of cedar and piñon and deep pine forests, of lazy river or white-water torrent; of broad valleys, twisting canyons, and towering mountains."

Monument Rock, Santa Fe. [pre 1915; $3-4]
From the back: "This rock, situated about 10 miles from Santa Fe, is in a deep gorge known as Santa Fe Canyon, the scenery of which is of incomparable beauty and grandeur…connects Santa Fe with Las Vegas."

Camel rock on Highway 285, near Santa Fe. [Circa 1940s; $1-3]
From the back: "Nature, the great sculptor, has fashioned rocks into many fantastic shapes and forms resembling human beings and animals but nowhere has she done anything more realistic than this Camel Rock just along side highway No. 285 about 13 miles north of Santa Fe, New Mexico. Here, for centuries this lifelike portrayal of a camel lying down looks forever toward of the north over a waste of un-watered soil, scrub, pine, and cedar."

Rio Grande Canyon. [Circa 1940; $6-8]
The Pueblo Indians called it *Posoge* (big river). It has also been known at various times as *Río de Nuestra Señora* (River of Our Lady), *Río de Nuestra Señora de la Concepción* (River of out Lady of the Conception) and the *Río Guadalquivir,* the River of May, the *Río Bravo* (in modern Mexico it is still known by that name, *bravo* meaning "wild," "turbulent," "restless," and sometimes "mean"). Juan de Oñate is thought to have been the first to call it the Rio Grande, and being the fourth longest river in the U.S., the name fits.

Hermit's Peak, Santa Fe Trail. [Circa 1920s; $2-4]
From the back: "The huge mountain lying to the north of Highway 85, near Las Vegas and neighboring towns, the traveler can see for many miles the reclining head, formed by the entire bulk of the mountain rising from the evergreen forest."

Rio Grande Canyon Road between Santa Fe and Taos. [pre 1915; $1-3] It is a wild, lonely drive between Santa Fe and Taos, marked by sheer perpendicular cliffs on one side and the canyon of the Rio Grande on the other. The scenery is breathtaking, different around each turn.

[Circa 1920s; $2-4]

Upper Pecos Valley, Santa Fe. [Circa 1950s; $1-2]
This card shows a picturesque, surprisingly verdant river valley. The Pecos River Valley is twenty miles long and encompasses some 223,667 acres of wilderness in the Sangre de Cristo Mountains.

Skiing in the Sangre de Cristo Mountains, Santa Fe. [Circa 1940s; $3-4]
From the back: "Most winter sports enthusiasts are surprised to learn that there is good skiing in sunny New Mexico. The high peaks of the Sangre de Cristo range afford good practice runs of varying degrees. Skiing is fast becoming popular at all points in New Mexico as well as Arizona."

Desert Flora

A common misconception among those unfamiliar with desert ecology is that a lack of water often constitutes a lack of life—that if a place is a desert, it is a dried out, barren wasteland filled with nothing but dust, rocks, and the occasional cactus. This is largely untrue, and even the most barren and dry desert is home to some form of life. The flora and fauna of the desert have found ways to exist without the abundance of water, and the desert abounds with life if a person knows where to look.

The area around Santa Fe has a particular abundance of plant life. Most obvious are the cacti, which range in size from the massive saguaro to the tiny pin cushion cactus. Sage brush and other desert grasses cover the ground, and the distinctive silhouette of the saguaro stands out on the horizon. During the spring and summer months, plants like the Great Plains yucca (the state flower of New Mexico), the ocatillo cactus, and the Century Plant display blooms of surprising color and size.

Santa Fe is also home to the Santa Fe National Forest, one of five National Forests in New Mexico.

Flora of the desert Southwest. [Circa 1940s; $1-2]
The desert Southwest is alive with flora—of every hue. Desert flowers are particularly fragrant, as an evening stroll will attest.

Ocotillo Cactus. [Circa 1940s; $1-2]
From the back: "Fouquieria Splendens, also called Candlewood, Coach-whip Cactus, and Jacobs Staff, at times appears as dry sticks only. The rainy season causes it to flame with slender, brilliant red panicles of bloom. Many southwestern hillsides are literally covered with this spiny shrub."

Barrel Cactus. [Circa 1940s; $1-2]
As shown in the picture, the barrel cactus always flowers from the top, and while the fruit is not normally considered edible, the flowers were used for food by Native Americans. In fact, all parts of the plant were used: the body was hollowed out and used as a cooking vessel, and even the spines were used for sewing.

Desert in bloom. [Circa 1940s; $1-2]
There are more than twenty species of the Cholla cactus in the deserts of the American Southwest. The bloom of the cholla is orange or greenish-yellow flowers in a variety of hues. They bloom April through June, depending on local conditions.

Rainbow Cactus. [Circa 1940s; $1-3]
From the back: "There are several varieties of Rainbows, among them the E. dasyacanthus or Texas Rainbow, E. chioranthus of New Mexico, and E. rigidissimus of Arizona, all noted for their varied and attractive blooms."

This image, taken from an original oil painting by the noted cowboy artist and poet, L.H. "Dude" Larsen, depicts a view of the desert Southwest that may exist only in the imagination. The front verse: "Enchanting is the desert lure / of our great southwestern / range / where peace and rest awaits you / where the seasons never change." [Circa 1940s; $1-2]

[Circa 1940s; $1-2]

Desert flora. [pre 1920; $2-4]
Flowers of the desert Southwest are particularly colorful in the early morning hours and in the evening, when their glorious colors seem to glow.

Many varieties of cacti. [Circa 1940; $1-2]
From the back: "The southwest has man varieties of cacti peculiar to the desert region only. It is strange that all vegetation has thorns as though a protection against an enemy. Many sections have an abundance of brush or small trees, such as Palo Verde, mesquite, greasewood, and sagebrush, all fortified with thorns."

Cholla Cactus. [Circa 1940s; $1-2]
The fiery colors of the Cholla Cactus add to the amazing vistas of the American Southwest.

Yucca, flower of the desert. [Circa 1940; $1-2]
The Yucca cactus, although native to the desert Southwest, has been adapted into the landscapes of homes all over the United States. Its stately bloom has been variously called "Spanish Bayonet," "Lamparas de Dios, " and Soapweed." From the back: "The Yucca with its beautiful panicle of waxen bells is a familiar sight in the foothills of the desert. 'God's Candle,' as it was named by the early Californians, grows from six to ten feet tall and the unique wood is often used for novelties."

Works Cited

Fergusson, Erna. *Dancing Gods: Indian Ceremonials of New Mexico and Arizona*. Alfred A. Knopf. New York, 1931.

King, Lesley S. *Frommer's New Mexico, 6th Edition*. IDG Books Worldwide, Inc. Foster City, 2001.

Milner, Clyde; Carol A. O'Connor; Martha A. Sandweiss, ed. *The Oxford History of the American West*. Oxford University Press. New York, 1994.

"Puye Cliff Dwellings." http://www.hanksville.org/voyage/misc/puye.html. 12/15/05.

"Santa Fe Walking Tour Background." Santa Fe Scene. http://santafescene.com/walking-tour/background.htm. 12/13/05.

"Visiting Santa Fe/Culture/History." Santa Fe Convention and Visitors Bureau. http://santafe.org/Visiting_Santa_Fe/Culture/History/index.html. 12/13/05.